ALAMO THEORY

DISCARD

JOSH BELL

Alamo Theory

COPPER CANYON PRESS

Port Townsend, Washington

Cover art: Kyle Thompson, *Untitled*

Copper Canyon Press is in residence at Fort Worden State Park in Port Townsend, Washington, under the auspices of Centrum. Centrum is a gathering place for artists and creative thinkers from around the world, students of all ages and backgrounds, and audiences seeking extraordinary cultural enrichment.

LIBRARY OF CONGRESS
CATALOGING-IN-PUBLICATION DATA

Names: Bell, Josh, 1971– author.
Title: Alamo theory / Josh Bell.
Description: Port Townsend, Washington : Copper Canyon Press, 2016.
Identifiers: LCCN 2015039061
ISBN 9781556593994
Classification: LCC PS3602.E64546 A6 2016 | DDC 811/.6 — dc23
LC record available at http://lccn.loc.gov /2015039061

9 8 7 6 5 4 3 2

FIRST PRINTING

Copper Canyon Press
Post Office Box 271
Port Townsend, Washington 98368
www.coppercanyonpress.org

CONTENTS

ALAMO THEORY

Dollar Dollar Bill

One more Jacobean kiss
and you'll wind up related to me.
One more emotion
and I'm coming for you, like a sparrow.
Set your phenomenology
on the windowsill.
Filthy, meet Family. Family,
I want to get marketable again.
In the meantime, what are your thoughts
on a completely male garden?
As little closure, maybe, as there is
a permanence? This being, also, the time
of the wandering Miss Americas.
Loose thumb-bones, rattling
in a mint tin. One more emotion
and both Dakotas will explode.
One more condition
and I'll be exiting my relevance.
And what was it, finally,
so dead about him, Family?
I think I just saw a fox.
Yes, with its little foxen teeth,
like Ezekiel's. Of course, you were off busy,
revising your plague journals.
Bringing clock to the beltline
of Orion. What could've you done

about the remaining days
no longer outnumbering us?
Voice of the dying groupie
like a deck of cards being shuffled.
One last electromagnetic pulse,
one last electromagnetic pulse,
and the neutral bodies of the dead
dropping from our larger, living bodies.
The truth? I thought the castration threat
a touch on the heavy side of the tonality.
But you got your point across.
And by then, we were a much
cleaner people, anyway.

Alamo Theory

Night falling once like a horse
through a bridge. Page God
refusing to be survived. Page God
hollering over one dirty haystack
at whoever's hiding behind the next
dirty haystack, and no one's getting
off this tractor alive, no one without
a pod of vanilla, stuck like a witch's
finger in the throat. Often who goes
there isn't the bees. Isn't the cherry trees.
No one's darker than me. No one's
big enough for pogroms. No one's
grammar gets a pass. Can't you
hear the popping of the karen-gun?
Why the Hittites, why the Etruscans,
sore and lost between vast greatness?
See the mountains, their trauma halos
of power line? Okay now show me
your anagram. No I don't even care.
We bury a prom dress in the sand
of every coast; sew a new prom dress
from the flag of every coast. Jesus
sat down, calmly, fashioned himself
a whip of leathern cord. Page God
had never recorded premeditation
at such levels. We never really learned

the correct usage of the voice box,
either, but when we took ourselves
by the neck, it was ancient, our language,
brave the living mammal pinned
to its duration, the problem with the orgy
always witness, witness, witness.
Your breath comes out in a pretty
cloud of blue, which is a different color
than most people use. What a brand-
new giveaway. Students of the game
have noticed that often, before I shoot,
I take the time to mention vegetation
fretting somewhere across a fact-lit
red hill. It's getting late and I'm the only
American on the dance floor. Still.

Josh II: The Return of Josh

We thought it walked a lot like Josh, clean white shirt down the soybean rows and toward us at the tree line, Josh walking through a field so green and real it made us feel like getting married just to look at it. Except for how the cricket-sound had moved inside of us, the crickets stopped their buzzing as he walked, and we took our eyes off Josh for a second, cows on fire in the pasture neighboring the soybean field, saw them crashing, tallow and sulfur, into golden hay bales. Again we turned our eyes to Josh, and we really thought it walked a lot like Josh, closer now, coming through the rows, with two large birds (this was strange) braiding what looked to be a length of red ribbon into his hair. Of course he was still a pretty good ways off—close enough that we could hear him singing, and I thought it sang a lot like Josh—but it was still just a little ways off now and the ribbon was a thin red ribbon and I couldn't say for sure it was a ribbon. So I asked Earl about the ribbon and Earl said *Ribbon,* and I asked Kim about the ribbon and Kim said *Ribbon,* and we agreed the ribbon made us feel like getting married just to look at it. And we agreed it walked a lot like Josh, except for now it was crawling, vines poking through the cloth of its pants legs like insect feelers, and we asked the ribbon birds to keep their eyes on Josh, and likewise we kept our eyes on Josh, or at least we thought that they were eyes: it was getting late, they worked like eyes, they followed Josh, and we felt the ribbon birds were on our side in all of this, that our parents would be calling to us soon, that the streetlights would be flickering on in the neighborhoods behind us, and Josh still closer, holding out his hands and opening his mouth as if he'd ask a favor, and I thought it would be smart if we could all agree upon an answer. So I asked Earl about the answer, and Earl said *Answer,* and I asked Kim about the answer, and Kim said—and this was just before we learned the truth about the ribbon—Kim said: *I don't think that's Josh.*

Vince Neil Meets Josh in a Chinese Restaurant
in Malibu (after Ezra Pound)

Back when my voice box
was a cabinet-full of golden vibrators, and my hair
fell white across the middle of my back
like a child's wedding dress,
I made love to at least a dozen girls
dressed up to look like me: the hotel bed a sky
filled with the flock
of our south-flying mic scarves,
the back of my head and the front
appearing simultaneously
in hotel mirrors, and the twin crusts of our makeup
sliding off into satin
like bits of California coast. I heard my own lyrics
coming out of the tent
of their beautiful wigs, my lyrics driven back
toward me, poled into me, demanding of me
the willing completion of vague circus acts
I'd scribbled down, once, on the back of a golf card
or a piece of toilet paper. Sometimes I myself
wonder what I was thinking then, but those words
went on to live forever, didn't they, radioed out
into the giant midwestern backseat
and blasted into kneecaps and tailbones
by that endless tongue of Berber carpeting

blanketing the American suburbs, boys and girls
strung like paper lanterns from here to Syracuse
along my microphone cord. Who rocks you now
rocks you always, I told them all,
and all of them somehow wearing
a homemade version of the same leather pants
I'd chosen to wear onstage that night;
all of them hoping to enter me — to enter anyone —
the way they thought I entered them,
and the way I entered them was wishing
I was somewhere else, or wishing I was
the someone else who'd come along
to enter me, which was the same thing. Love
in battle conditions requires a broad
taxonomy, queerness has its ever-more-visible degrees.
Josh, I know you know what I'm talking about,
you have the build of a stevedore. Which reminds me,
as a child in Nanjing,
I sculled the junks for my bread and I slept
in a hovel along the Chiang Jiang River.
I bred mice in a cage there who built their nests
from the frayed rope I'd taken from the decks, and one spring,
when the babies did not emerge, I lifted
up the rock that hid them, and I found
they'd grown together, fused with each other
and the tendrils of the nest. I held them up, eleven blind tomatoes
wriggling on a blackened vine. And now you come to me
in this Chinese restaurant in Malibu,

asking if you can help me. Please tell *Circus Magazine* I love them truly, and please pass Pamela this message:
If you get back to Malibu by springtime, drop by the houseboat, and I'll rock your ass as far as Cho-fu-Sa.

Where the I Comes From

Our days often ended and began
with the sound of voices raised
in song. Even after we murdered
our friends and neighbors. Even
after we brought the attention
of our knives to the neighbors of
our neighbors, until at last
the neighborhoods fell silent
and the cities quiet and the city's
city, the country then and next
the country, until finally the moon,
as if its own reflection, looked
upon an Earth that we had emptied
nearly back to Eden. Even then,
in that silence that seemed almost
a silence, sadly we were not
alone. All we ever wanted was
to be alone, to visit no one, to be
visited by nothing. But even after
we'd traveled to the nearby planets
and relieved them of their voices,
even after—and we all knew
this was coming—we fell amongst
each other, brother and sister,
until only I survived, still I heard it,
the universe subtracted of its skin

and hair, and yet the sound
of a voice, like someone singing
in the hold of a sinking ship,
unbidden and irrelevant, a fathom
and a fathom deep, but never fading.

If Not Princess, Then Warden

Things start off well: I'm the warden and no one's writing on the walls in shit. I encourage all inmates to grow a mustache like mine, a bit of sculpted punctuation curling beneath the nose, directing the reader of the face downward to the lips. With them, and to the fellow in the mirror, I say, "my sweat unbreakable you," helplessly using the word *sweat* instead of *sweet*, the way a high-school girlfriend did once in a letter, writing "Sweatheart, are we still going to the jamboree?" We were not going to the jamboree, anymore, Sally Garrett. This morning, out by the smokestacks before school, Lisa Shields pulled a bent cigarette out of the left cup of her bra before fishing for her father's Zippo lighter amidst the rubble of an ancient civilization forgotten in the chaos of a giant orange purse. I peek into the purse, around the rotating axletree of Lisa's searching arm, past the anthropologists dusting for fingerprints on a greasy tube of lipstick, and see a scene from the future reflected in a silver hand mirror: my English teacher, Mrs. Little, sitting on her desk while she explains how it wasn't her intention to pigeonhole me as a poor student, except instead of the word *pigeonhole,* which I know she means to use, she keeps saying *cornhole,* not recognizing her mistake: "I never meant to cornhole you," she says, again and again, "It was not my intention to cornhole you," until I am dizzy, and when her black Mary Jane drops from her left foot to the classroom floor, where it will never move again unless someone picks it up and runs with it, I pick it up and run. For twenty years I have kept this shoe incarcerated, in solitary confinement, in the deepest level of the prison. These days, when I fear a riot—shivs like needlefish in toilet after toilet, the shrieks of the pigeonholed bursting from the prison library—I descend the steps to take my visitation with the shoe, but try as I might, I cannot make it fit my dick. And it's always at this moment, that standing close to me, before school, Lisa glances down at the ill-fitting shoe, then lights her father's Zippo with a pop that also seems to bring to life a chainsaw somewhere in the subdivision behind us. "It seems you're not Cinderella, after all," she will go on to say to me, in the shadow of the smokestacks. But until she does, I stand there, preparing myself to believe her, thinking of the jamboree, Sweetheart, and planning the cruel mustache of the future.

Pensées of the Sucker MC

See the shining city on the hill? Most of their laws
have to do with crops
and sorcerers. City attractive
as a first responder. City good at everything
like the she-male. When the owl
had a dollar bill inside of it,
when the plague had yet to make
its way to a theodicy, I stood on the steps
of the courthouse, saying truly
that sentiment is fear. Sexual partner,
sometimes your address
is your only remains. Sexual partner,
gone to the outlying vineyards
and the cellar invisible, gone
into the whistle and the metal
of the whistle. Meanwhile, my fellows, they tie
my eyes to a rough-hewn board. They payroll
my bones and rain their curses
down upon me, as if a rain of come.
Even those born before me
shall outlive me. Even those born after me
shall exceed my consequence.
On the hill, a city, and in the city, a house.
And someday you will all be sorry
when you recall how carefully
I closed each door behind me.

The Last Critique

We think Elizabeth's poems suck. We think Steve's poems suck. And we think Rachel's poems suck Elizabeth's poems. We didn't remember how or why the Stranger's poems sucked, but we thought Holly was good, so it scared us when the Stranger's poems refused to suck Holly's poems. A lot of people want to suck Fred's new poems, which suck, but they are too difficult for us to suck, and we'd rather suck his old ones, for though they are old, and suck, it is much easier to suck them. When she reads them out loud, Clarise's poems suck pretty good, but we are reserving our final judgment until we've seen them sucking on the page. We think Martha's poems suck. Sometimes when we think we're sucking on one of Theodore's poems, we're actually sucking on two. We think Ed's poems have that Girl Scout look, which makes us want to start a family when we hear them through the keyhole, sucking. Philbert's poems suck like they've been sucking Annie's poems too much. Annie's poems sucked, but at least they brought something new to the act of sucking, we'd never seen a poem sucked like that before, and we thrilled to suck on them, as if sucking on household appliances. Many people enjoy the austere sucking of Terry's poems. Still, no one pays to suck Terry's poems like they pay to suck Anton's. We think Tom-Tom's poems suck *so* hard. We think Wendy's mature poems suck near the unassailable power of the Stranger's poems, and at first we are frightened, as if forced to suck an entire opera, when Wendy gets that Viking look and makes us suck her poems. Maybe we could arrange for Terry's poems, Wendy will say, to suck the Stranger's poems, but the Stranger's poems are missing, and Terry is afraid, and we do not blame him, as some of us recall the first time we heard the Stranger's poems, which *enter* sucking bird and beast and flower, sucking queen and beggar, Oldsmobile and go-kart, saying long-time-no-suck-me, saying Terry: suck Wendy, suck Holly, saying suck the redwood forest, saying suck me lonely mannequin, saying suck the abundant splendored thrice jismatic suck of lonely mannequin, saying suck theology, missile launch, stirrups and ballet. Some of us choose to recall, instead, how the Stranger's poems seemed capable of sucking themselves, as if they no longer required us to suck them, and filled with obsolescence we had to run next door to suck our neighbor's poems, real quick. But we all agree on the way, when the Stranger's poems end, they appear to suck the entire round planet, all at once, the planet which — in the Stranger's poem's unhinged jaws — comes dressed up like the Bride who was a Sailor, but all in the white of clouds and with a metallic S&M rig peeking through underneath, showing the chaste girdle of skyscrapers inside of which we suck and sleep and suck the poems we've written in fear of sucking the Stranger's poems, which go on sucking hard for us, through the disastered warp of Time, the Stranger's poems uncanonized, built to be sucked in a way we will never understand, as the Stranger's poems are a work of genius, and only our children's children will ever fully suck them.

Here Are Some Problems I Have with Your Wife

I

She's a lot more fluent in Portuguese
than she used to be. Holds hands with all
my ex-girlfriends, who afterward seem
so much taller. And later, as I blew out
my candles, she said to those gathered, *I'll bet
he wished to be sodomized by thieves.*
Your wife comes from a family of thieves.
Her mother taught her never to confuse
sex with the doing of one's taxes. I'll get
to her father later. Her father is a series
of furnaces. About your wife's novel I wrote,
Friends, this is the worst birthday party, ever.
She took it as a compliment. Love, kill,
betray, deify, vote for, nap with, or bury alive?

II

She changed her telephone number.
She doesn't have any birds inside of her.
Her idea becomes flesh by early afternoon.
When I first read your wife's new memoir,
Sir, it felt like watching the lighthouse
go dark, like doing inventory, finding one
planet missing. No doubt your wife knows
very well which planet. I look forward to
your next dinner party, where I may sample

from the catered board, ask your wife
about said memoir. Last time I read it, I awoke
to find myself burning heretics. I guess
what it is, is that probably your wife puts
her allotted birds inside of other people.

III

Your wife's police are a very special
kind of police. They fingereth the apple
of mine eye, and there are way too many
testicles to count. Likewise, this is a strange-
looking bed. And this is a magic handkerchief.
You wish it were eighteen horseflies. You wish
your wife's police were far more brutal. Me,
I never bought the premise that your wife
was ever a girl, but if I did, I wouldn't
take it personally. I'm not a nest of living
wig-hair, nor baby-bits, nor eighteen flies pouring
from the mouth of whoever's hiding in this
weird new bed with me. Come out, Inflatabilium.
Don't make me call your wife's police.

Vince Neil Accompanies Josh to Luncheon with Scholars, Poets, and Others – Gets Cell Phone Number of Grad Student Sitting at Far End of Table – Orders Cheeseburger, No Tomato – Borrows Josh's Cell Phone – Calls Grad Student Sitting at Far End of Table

If I'd been born a girl, like you,
I wouldn't have lived any longer than I will,
and whether I'd be waiting
in my new long johns, or in the plus-size version
of your blouse and Target pumps,
still the ancient Boy Scout Death would sidle up
and find me in the houseboat,
compliment my penmanship, my knots, and then
he'd lead me to the minivan, never to be seen
with this hairstyle again, the handsome scalp
and blond fringe now worn
by seagulls, who hit the high notes like it was nothing,
who think in unison, though they never
seem to fly that way, instead go dropping singular
from the squiggled flock
after bread crust and fish eye, blip-blip
down from the sky, rogue threads of EKG. I mean to say
what's globbed is globbed for good
and even John Keats will not unfuck it for us.
Though maybe you have this feeling
about me – good! – and maybe then
you paste that feeling down with words
and I do the same, and then dreaming in our beds

we get the lonely message from each other,
just in time, just as the jackbooted soldiers
come rushing in, over the picket fence, with every fourth beat
of the fearful heart gone pulsing out its tracer bullet
into a potholed DMZ of sky—I'm not sure
what your dreams are like—the moon
now a cross section of bludgeoned tomato
over the schoolhouse, and now a white pants button
lost on the highway asphalt. Learning is strictly
for girls, the guns still going chop-chop-chop,
and John Keats, in those remaining years,
he kept sending up his test obituaries
like weather balloons, poems still floating even now
over Tulsa and the like, their comely
bivalve pentameter interfering
with radio signals, just the reverse
of the way a beautiful, living body
can scan so vibrantly it zones out
all the ghost code, can get between me
and the important messages
I should be getting from the underworld,
one code for another, the dead only interfering
with the living who've interfered
with the dead, and along those lines
I really think I'd be suspicious
of that veggie plate if I were you. It's strange
how rarely the meat they serve us
resembles an animal, and strange how the vegetables,
despite their cleanliness and grace, so often do:

a tail or torso of zucchini, and once I saw a rat-shaped eggplant
hunched feral in a kitchen off Hermosa.
Look to the sea, as usual, for echoes:
of course the many benthic cousins
of the turnip, spindly fruits morphing up their bodies
for our inspection in unsounded caves
filled with various see-through creatures
easily mistaken for prostitutes,
and finally the Sirens plugging up their ears
against what new songs we have to offer.
My latest begins with a simple verse
about the girl with one lung and one gill,
how she loved me, how she sang
and how I never kissed her more than twenty feet
away from a swimming pool, how
she answered the phone and how
her phone voice made me feel
like running away to the forest, rebuilding
the old tree house, then interrogating
the lilies of the field. And I promise you,
whatever your name is, I'm going to ride this feeling
all the way to Target. Because eventually all voices cease,
and—if I've been reading these poems right—
there's a hand job waiting for us in the clouds.

PSA

If you're a little girl—and if you're reading this, we're pretty sure you are—then there's a good chance you're going to have your body taken over by a spirit, one trapped between this world and the next, tenant or tenants counting on your skin as a way to feel the world again, which is a funny thing to think of, someone missing the world, the world where no one arrives for the tea party and thoughts are still kept locked in heads. But possession is standard in your case, and nothing to be embarrassed about. So into the playroom you go, as yourself for some while longer, lucky with your left eye slowly filling up with dolls. When we were living children, we had the dream in which the spirit would come for us, like a tornado, would guard our body in the ice and vacuum of its eye, the meat like insulation for the floating wire of our skeleton, along which would flow the charge that brings the invisible world into the present, the place of church and fingernails, leaving us vivid, smoking as circuit, rivulets of sizzling fat. And then we would have been so like you, and then we would have been quite necessary, and we kept our faces hidden and we waited, and then no spirit ever came.

American History

How we loved your pork chops, fell out of carriages
to love them. When time was a problem. At first how cautiously, but then how many

and how often. Why we broke into their bones
like they were banks, tossed our plunder to the river's

bloated crib. How we loved your pork chops, dreamed them sliced by rising helicopter blades
from a pink strip of daybreak, saw them drop like stone tablets into soy fields

and how the helicopters followed, dropping like banks into soy fields
the green of dental floss. Wherein we watched ourselves in hand mirrors, eating your pork chops

and claiming your pork chops loved us back. How you left so many bodies behind
when time was a problem. Or why the famous artists of the age

painted their own faces over ours, sitting at your dinner table
where they had never been. Why we knew why. How it was never you who cooked

your pork chops, then served them to the faces. Back when you evolved
from the vicinity of bone to the clean gristle of weeds,

were graduated to your broken meal of ash and black thistle,
were the last vegetarian. Then how you flew like scarecrows across

the smokeless palate of the desert, disappeared beyond the cloying ligament
and pretense of all food. Where you fell like a bank and left so many beautiful

bodies behind you. Why time was a problem. Why we arrived late for funerals,
carrying our dusty silverware on a belt of green dental floss,

and whosoever's at a loss for shovels, dig. How we loved your pork chops
and indivisibly how. Why we navigated by the glow of their grilling,

burst into a million moths when we ran afoul of headlights,
loved your pork chops through the prescription and the plaster, broke out of hospitals

to love them, came back in time machines just to watch ourselves
breaking out of hospitals to love them. When time was a problem. How jealous

we became of our past selves, handsome at the distant dinner table
where we could no longer touch the lovely pork chops

we'd gotten ugly touching. Why we wanted to see the new pork chops,
the pork chops raw, so broke into your kitchen for a glimpse of them,

pink tomahawks we'd thwack into the mouths of how many mouths
it was we finally had when the dogs finally reached us. In

the time when time was a problem and the mouth a currency,
then did we imagine long days without silverware, when still your pork chops

somehow kept our thoughts from the epiphany of the intricate
and candled skeletons of pig. And how you left a lot of beautiful bodies behind

but nothing like those last ones. Why we broke into their bones
like children will, and when we saw that you would no longer allow us

to love your pork chops anymore, then why we marched them to the green soy fields
and fixed it so that no one else would love them.

Your Prime Minister Speaks

All night long I think I've been wearing a certain hat. I've had my dinner, met with the Secretary of Wheat, watched the news on television, all the while wearing this certain hat, my favorite hat, you know the one, gold rope and no feathers, made famous in the famous portrait of me, hanging in the State Museum. Sitting here at my desk, signing my name to important papers, I can close my eyes and picture myself as I truly am: there's my hat, and there's my head inside it: pale, cradled like a baby, rocking above the important papers I am signing, and everything is as I have imagined it, time immemorial. But by now it should be obvious to you, as it is not obvious to me, that I am actually wearing a different hat altogether. A good hat, yes. A fine hat, true. But not the one I *think* I'm wearing, not my favorite hat, the one made famous in the famous portrait of me, which, for all I know, is still hanging in the museum, the museum that is, for all I know, still standing. So when I put down my pen and walk into the bedroom for a nap and see the hat I think I'm wearing, not on my head but tossed off and half-hidden in the bedclothes, you must forgive me (I am still your Prime Minister, after all) if for a second I believe I've been beheaded.

One Night in His Hotel Room, Vince Neil Reads Aloud His
"Open Letter to the Men and Women of Malibu, Who May No
Longer Love Me as They Have," a Nice Bit of Writing about
Which Josh Offers Very Little in the Way of Criticism

Put your good teeth in tonight, Malibu.
This is not the letter where
I look for answers in the underworld, nor the one
where I subdue the local monster
or reenergize the phrase
white love. Too often I have awakened
beneath the sticky-fingered dawn
with the furniture acting like it thinks
no one is watching, too often I have eaten roots
to survive, have paid attention
to a ghostly counsel, and so it is my thesis
that the West is safely answered for. Instead,
I have come here to ask you
your forgiveness, for having lived
as long as I have lived
inside this present body. There's nothing
wrong with it. I gave it to you
and it worked. I put new holes in it,
tried to keep it wrapped
in skin, overstayed the welcome of it
which was mine to give, and when in port
whittled proclamation
on its hull. White love,

white love, it isn't like I want
to live forever, and do I even care
for that type of immortality
where I should feel
the comfort of my voice, as it sails on
without me, toward an undifferentiated
forever of cover bands
and ringtone? What good is the deathless
morseling out of memory, through works,
to me that made it? Once I am dead
I will no longer pay for cable
or for sex. No more, after porn,
will I contemplate the void. Our Josh
once tried to write some elegies
for friends of his who were still alive, in case
his powers failed him or he died. No
such luck. Beauty is the soft beginning
of a long interrogation. The dirt is a younger
plagiarist, tossing up the new bodies
out of coffee grounds, presidents,
and fluorescent lights, so few of the freshly congregated
making a sound we haven't
yet heard. When I wore the ponytail
in the shower, back when the entire world
was a blond, I'd reach back to wring
the water from it, and it felt dense back there
where it should have been dead, seemed
serpentine and alive. What's my name,
I would ask of it, tugging, what's my name? Malibu,

your boys are thin and tan, like rigging.
Tonight, your women are never
sleeping over, but I am not jealous of their whereabouts
in the parochial way of speaking. All I want
is to fly at them, who've known me,
wearing a strange face, breaking in the logic
of the new shape, to redeem myself
like a soldier or a nun. Though even if I were presented
in an unexpected body, there still would be
that final problem of the mind, unchangeable, geologic
where it should be lit. Creaturely it crawls
toward its favored
beacons, in the muck. Its regrets and jealousies return
and accrue, a sideshow host pitching its tents
against the battlements, round about. The habit,
the callous, the sublime. The temple of the Lord,
the temple of the Lord, the temple of the Lord
are these. I said *geologic,* Josh, because
our time on Earth is limited by rocks
and scientists. Yet it is even worse,
sometimes, that when a woman turns to hold me,
it is *my* body—not the bodies of others
she has held, or will—it is my own body
that I first grow jealous of. The faith has taught me
how this, my flesh, is not my own, but since
it is a thing, then it is a possession,
and since a girl is holding it
she isn't holding me. You have had this feeling
if you have ever ordered the special

in a restaurant, or said the reverent words, such as *coral*
and *depilatory,* then saw them floating gossamer
into someone else's ears, where they
go on to make their residence. The body
is a problem. Not that I believe
that I have to be this endless thing inside myself, undoable filament
in a buckling cabinetry of flesh.
To get to that point, if they do not counsel God
or art, the balladeers have referred us
to love, but it's the how we'll make
our way, with love, that I don't believe,
old chemistry set, made up of the cherished
and available bodies, and which sluice
or compound, what accident of mutual respect,
rottweiler, finger-fuck, and valentine
to attack the cell phone tower and expert
circuitry of death? I have never lived in a house
with a cellar, and if I had a daughter
I'd keep her far from words. Entire lexicons
in betrayal, their syllables picked up
and kept on running through the other mouths
long after they are done with ours,
our mouths are just a proof, the residue, that documents
their use. But don't revoke my sainthood yet.
I was listening to Prince when I wrote all of this.
For this is the body that will be
forever body: and this is the word, *elevator,*
which shall be chaste, and mine, from here on out:
sometimes, walking away after descending

a great height from an elevator, I still
can feel — through a mistake of the inner ear —
the mechanism pulling at me,
from below, as if it would like, even on the street
outside the hotel, to bring me living,
through the asphalt, to the fires. I can't
stay away from the underworld. I will never have
the molecules. Malibu, with your trick
pelvis. Malibu, a city, a mouth always tasting
as if washed out with soap, possibly
by your own hand. The cult of romantic love
arises from this context — where we are
pure as the bacteria we murder — and forgets the mortal ligature
that comes along with a sunrise
that is busy tying off the bedposts, the zilch
of metaphysics, and as for any love notes
you might be sending me
in the future, please make them
sincere, obscene, and grammatically correct.
As for God and song, I am susceptible,
once dreamed, in another draft of this letter,
that the tree bark and the ocean skin
would favor my reentry. But what has to be done
will have to be done in the current body,
even though I am unable
to name what ails it, to place its needs
into words, I sometimes catch myself wanting to be handled
by a very talented and perverse
kind of veterinarian, one who can tell the matter

without me saying where it hurts. I am
about postverbal now. In the peroration we may require
something Greek, Josh, like a reference
to Herodotus or sodomy. We may need something natural,
too, like sodomy and birds. We try so hard,
after death, to keep clothing
on the beloved's body, but the body
keeps disrobing, simply won't behave. Through the earth
it goes sailing, in full compliance to fine wind
always, and I, too, once felt chosen, did I not, by fate and friendship
and the like, thought I had managed
my life fairly well: nervous in a larger crowd, true,
but well at ease within all denominations
of the threesome, always searching out
that half-erected subdivision of beauty
which is not a joy forever. And recently, on vacation
surf casting down in Baja, I accidentally
snagged a purple inner tube
with a small blond child at play within, and imagined
as I reeled her in she was the daughter
of myself and an oceanic platinum beast, one rising
male and female from the drink
as if by elevator, chain-mailed with sea fleas,
its shoe color and heel length changing
as each wave broke, a capitalism
of plenty and regret. First floor: swimwear
and the tears of heroes. That day I reeled the punctured
inner tube and frightened child to shore
for her parents to collect, signed my autograph, as apology,

to their actual T-shirts, and sent them
on their way. Children fight hard
but you cannot keep them. And if you're ever
feeling confused or lonely,
Malibu, just call Josh up
on the cell: 617-388-3591. If no one answers, please
leave a message for me there, perhaps listing
your convictions. All those with genitalia
shall believe; all those without
will be more talented, and I will pay
to have them write the ending for me.

The Films of Tony Scott

Should a secretary sleep inside of Tony Scott? The biologist attends in him—why not?—as an arch attends upon opponent necrochemistry. Thereby raising yet another question: Should we imagine the grid will fail instead? For example: I allege a receiver, an unauthorized link. Then, after an existence, the gun borrows a small silver compact honoring the monocratic revolutionary, but it was the baby actress, cheating across the epic, and it is an independence that is associated with camera, not with when. Actress, come out, when invoked, with tetrahedron boots, for play. Thereafter, within that imperative, a sect: the given lamp: the satellite-peripheral whooping through the engine: the Tony Scott, the Tony Scott, the continental shouts, and the unseen damages to the bedframe, all night long, bulleting and graduate to anniversary nonsense, one camera injected under the converter, or to toe the line within the gun. Hips coast inside the gun. Eat, baby actress, now caught stacking money beneath her twentieth affair. Whoever compensates an instinct near the secondary appraisal is the actress, numeric manifesto in flux around her, carrying the groceries, the torches, the disease of all kinds, the ribbon-said alien that perceiveth her into something beneath her discipline. And it *is* beneath her discipline, for look: shot for shot the pilgrim-worker darts, the birthday-lawyer, a single, giant krill of dark, which is the Tony Scott, the Tony Scott, the attack, the contour, the surface-mummy carrying on through its more or less vulnerable alphabet. In closing, much of the here-incentive constrains the *I* above the maker. Therefore it is time to introduce you to the films of the famous Tony Scott, wed in the theme park of a tense species, table on the table, though something other than a meat.

We Will Begin by Placing You in This Bag

There's friend A, the totally sexy one.

And there's friend C, he made the sculpture of the ice cube for A, the totally sexy one.

We don't know where B has gotten to, B who is married to C, B probably out breaking
windows, writing a poem about how beauty is the knife.

D is not our friend, D the towheaded one, she knows us through B, but we are being nice
to D for now so maybe we can kiss her, D or B the poetess, whichever, so you can
help us keep our cover

at least until E shows up, with her unfinished spy novel and her can of olives

for G and us. G and us we like to sleep when it's raining

and eat olives, to hell with girls, and you be G for a while, we like you a lot, G, whoever
you are, so unlike F, forget about F, with his silly complaints and his too-finished
movie script, beginning with the phrase "We open on the void," that F,
strange F, we're starting to like F a little better now, yes F
is really starting to grow on us,

but we're telling you flat out we're in love with H, she wants to lick A's slender calves,
we always love such lesbians as are unavailable to us, and H is also thinking
about changing her name

to I, but we already have a friend named I, which I hates because it's

a girl's name, and I have come for the body of J

says K to J in the hallway. I have come for the body of K

booms M to K, looming up behind her, and L, who is standing behind *him,* slaps him
on the back of the head, she is so jealous

of K, but not as jealous as N is of A, the totally sexy one, N who is our girlfriend, our
girlfriend who went to prison with O, O of whom *we're* jealous, who writes us
letters from prison assuring us we *should* be jealous, saying sometimes

through the bars and in the prison yard the dew on the grass

looks like little diamonds

she can't steal. Did anyone see where J went? J knows us through P and P is standing

over there, trying to appear as if he is not wearing ladies' underpants, you'll

get so you can draw that expression from memory, but wait, that's not P

after all, we don't know who that is, P went home to New Hampshire and

anyway Q was not invited, what's she doing here?

Right there, standing at the punch bowl next to, wait a minute, is that R?

We think it is. R, how are you, you can barely see the scar, and S so handsome tonight

it makes T think of parakeets flying through

a scarf of rain, and U gets down on his knees before us all,

which makes V think he's going to say a prayer or make a pass at A, the totally sexy one, but it's

really that he's lost a contact lens, but which first thoughts V

confides to W, and that funny V, thinks W, always getting ecumenical, but is *ecumenical*

the right word? thinks X, reading everyone's thoughts, that is so like X, and then X says, as if it's

just hit her: "Is it me, or did someone actually say *scarf of rain?*"

and Y never shows up until late, and when she does come strolling through the door

she is exactly sixteen minutes pregnant

and Z, whose house this is, who is our gracious host, you can bet he makes a note of it.

Blue Safari

Or bring along an extra shovel
for me, a map of the area, some new
interferences, we may
need to plant something. Normally I'd leave
the important digging to you
because I am afraid of tools and how my fingers fall
to rest so easily on handles, of the earth
when it's been opened, and furthermore
I'm afraid to close it
when I'm done with it,
there are baby teeth down there, beetles
in the hollow of a doll's head. Though let me say
I am hardly ever done with it,
Earth, or whatever it was
the first ones called it, even when it's signaling
that it's done with me. The time line unwinds,
weeds firing up from the window box
like rockets, the rowboat sun
somewhat closer than recorded. Additionally
we may need to capture something
in advance of burying it: a wild animal,
a wild animal, I am almost certain
we have been commissioned to capture
a wild animal, ears like radar dishes
turning always toward the racket
we are making, despite how quiet we must be

stacking tools and tent-poles
in the bed of my pickup truck. Or at least
that's how I've drawn it
here in my sketchbook. Or first it was
the tools, and then it was our hands
were built for them, and they were built
with other tools entirely, over whose wooden bodies
and crooked metal heads
they never let us speak of the weather
or of the day our bodies will disappear, taking all their secrets
and favorite paintings along with them
toward the sun. Long and thin, your hands
are for the removing of beetles
from a doll's head, which is why
I am so happy you are here with me
even though you're far away,
it's just your voice on the cell phone
that confuses me. And as if I thought of it myself
I say this thing about your hands
but I had to read the story of them
on them, while you were walking down the street
and of their own accord
they spun your hair in pigtails. I always loved
that painting. You always got
a signal, even in the jungle. Also the photo of you
held here by static to the center of
my television screen, so that your face plays over
the roles that flicker there
behind it. On one channel, you take the stage

at the Apollo. On another, you're crying
because your husband's in a coma.
I'd like for you to take him
off the respirator — it's
the kindest thing to do — then bring yourself
and the respirator over here
to my house, we'll take it on
safari, don't forget to pack the respirator, or maybe on
a picnic, don't forget to pack
the blowgun and the radio, the one that plays
the song forever, the one
with the list of rejected names
for the planet Earth, the one with the darts made up
of Detroit steel, the one with the giant voice
and the pretty wraith inside, exactly
how many blowguns
do you have in there? Many radio signals
go all the way, clear into the root system
and the water table, where they pick up other trees
or reemerge as these giant flowers
we are busy hacking a path through
on the way to our room
at the Safari Diner Motel Inn. I love that picture of us
they hung above the coffeemaker:
forty is the new death
and we've been up all night dealing
with all the wrong satellites.

Penultimate Letter to Your Wife

Hetero-telepath, blister of num-num, first the thumb-suck, and then the codicil, and down the back stairs come to me, first-time voter, bones in Delta formation, come louche as dinosaur and please unconscious, make of thyself unconscious thing please, aka insensate, aka The Money-Truck, unseen by husband, cymbalist, go out of your way for me, like a Quaker, rubber bunny in that ugly muffin-hat or nothing but your hair-sleeves, abeat about your temple as in flags, excuse me I meant bunny-rubber, and all in a sleepwalk, no one should keep that many trout, busgirl, toothbrush holder, and to a longsome steely brig of moonlight come, raging cohort, vivisect for hollyhock, also that's a prayer mat not a wedding dress, not anymore a wedding dress, a lien against my holdings is your breathing, your cities engulfed in strife, you gave your blood away to build these many children, and corkscrew, wee dread-nought, I'm literally spanking the kitchen, Andalusia, infundibula, nice assonance, that nostalgia you're feeling is just my inner vacuum, though everyone's stealing my tools now, and my books, and drug yourself if need to, I don't want to be the one who drugs you this time, why won't you be proactive, sister of the pharmacist, becoming as a library, bring your body along with you, like a bedroll, into the yard, out behind your marital address, where I'm becoming a library, I've got an invisible baby that needs to take a shape in blood, outside now so you can use your fascist voice, jury of chipmunk, you and I will sleep on your dead body, hard to see two people sleeping on a dead body that belongs to one of the sleepers who also sleeps upon it, but hey it sometimes happens, like an underwater library I can't do anything about it, your husband using up all the Marxism, plus I think your children get their faces from his face, too bad for you, not going to send your face forward this time around, this was going to be a picnic, it's an archaeological exhibit, yes I'm finally thinking quaquaversally, so come to the lean-to, unclip that shadow, investment banker, longshoremistress, invisible baby, invisible baby in your blood.

Sci-Fi Violence

Would a true prophet use an electric
salamander as a tongue?
That's what I thought. Last rainfall
in the new city, held here
until we ship the wounded home,
the enemy collecting like aberrant
cells across the river.
Like me, they are afraid a rainbow
will notice and destroy them. Like me,
they were born believing
their body parts didn't
get fucked together right. Is it fate
we name? Is it countries? One enemy
in whom I planted sixteen seeds.
One enemy who attempted
to tongue-kiss my eyeholes, and two cakes
of arsenic tucked
beneath his armpits. Look
carefully around you, then return
your look to me. As with a small
percentage of my countrymen, I die if I sleep
in a horizontal position, sucky
little prostitute of muscle
in the chest. Pinned down
by guerrilla holdouts
in a rooftop dumpster, I think

of my imperial home,
of walking the orchard rows
with childhood friends, half of whom
I own, some of whom
have names. Each night, they'd tape me
upright to the wall, so that I could dream
safely in the vertical, as God
intended me to do. An elegy
is someone left alone, for hours,
in a room with a dead body. And there have always
been rules against that sort of thing.

While Josh Sleeps, Vince Neil Recites His "Love Song for Flight
Attendant on Continental Express 1147, to Austin, Texas"

I am a system of oppression
and you're a Scorpio, with Austin
coasting toward us as the shark, though all
we can really see from here
is a polar sheet of clouds, the world not round at all
as we've suspected, or in possession
of the manufactured edge, but flat alone
and going on forever, nothing up here
to walk across or screw a headboard to,
and I fear we won't be able
to maintain this level of honesty
with each other. People are listening. Depression
is the normal body, just the giant thing
strapped to g-forces, so hard
to lift one's head, and in the final analysis
I hate a cup of tea: it always tastes
like roots to me, and roots
are so proud, headed for the hidden sources
like scholarly experts, moving always farther
away from what they feed. You know
I didn't want, along with the earthward
mermaids, to honor my way
onto the beach, pectoral fins evolving
toward the better flag
of hands. Rather than that earth,

if we should break into it, I'd like to fall into the sea
from here, grow tails with you, return
to where fish robs fish
and the big snails move
ponderously, alone as automobiles
and far from grace, as we were told,
the word *salvation* not invented yet
nor the forfeiture of sound. Microbe and harness,
the ocean will not invent us, and (1) as I have said, honesty
is important, (2) in stature, yes, you are a very
tiny person, and yet, (3) you know how it is
with some sharks: younger
in testament, emergent conditions
in the water park, but never
leave a tooth behind. And so it is
I fantasize that I'm a smaller person
on airplanes, though history teaches us
that bodily confinements —
the tray stand, the void — sometimes lead to thought
and vision. Josh will tell you
if you ask him it was William Blake
who walked outside one day
and saw a tree, teeming with angels, and I think
Blake may have even thought
they were a pretty sight. I wouldn't have been so sure: hard
to tell an angel from a ghost:
both of them repositioning chains
in high branches, both extremely dedicated
to craft, both with the heavenly light

streaming out of their mouths, both utterly
and horribly dead. In truth I don't like flying at all
but not for the usual reasons: I think they should make flight
a more terrifying experience, the employment
of glass-bottomed planes, or pilots
reciting the Lord's Prayer, other bits
of inspirational verse, flight attendants
who pretend to hear me say
I have a bomb, come live with me
inside this bomb. But mostly I feel so vulnerable
with all these strangers looking
at the back of my head. I wish I had eyes
back there, but also a living nose, and a mouthful
of working teeth, though this of course
makes me wonder how it would feel
to kiss two women at once,
on both sides of my head, with the regular mouth
and the backup. You would be
such a conduit, the women sending messages
to each other through your skull, and since
you were the implement, you would never know
if they were telling lies about you
or just speaking intimately, like sisters:
who dig their tunnels through a hill
from both directions, meet in the middle
where they hold hands and collect grubs
and earthworms in a Holly Hobbie lunch box.
But I like it best, with the single mouth,
when the woman misjudges the spacing a bit,

then cracks into your teeth
with her teeth, like a shark hitting the cage, and this all well before
the underpants and the nicotine patches
hit the floor, you and your partner the known center
of the named tradition, the body's mystery unanswerable
(sweet, sweet lunch box)
yet completely exhaustible, the male
still the taller of the species, and not a different
kind of animal. There's an honesty, at least,
in these collisions, maybe just because
you get reminded of your skeleton, there beautiful
but hidden, so no one ever gets to see it
in the light, at least not during the parley
of affectionate conditions, its vision only sanctioned
by the body through a windshield
and later in the weird
flirtation of the trauma ward. When you
were just a kid, I rocked Austin
on back into Mexico, afterward walked the strip
without bodyguard, my tongue like a sheet of sandpaper
working the roof of my mouth
into a vaulted proscenium, the angelic orders
inscribed into the fish-scale patterns
of the hard palate, and I wished
to be small enough to stand
on the stage of my own tongue,
ping a couple of high notes off the new
acoustics, as it seemed sometimes—
as in the myth about the maiden changed to stone or bird—

that my voice would never end,
and the man stamping hands outside
the club I wound up in (Austin), did he not hold my hand
a little longer than necessary? Then look
into my eyes? He smelled like
a copy machine, the void rolling off of him
8½ × 11, and in that way
you kind of remind me of him. So when you finally take yourself away
to the other passengers, I'm going to hit
the call button, and you'll come walking back to me
down the narrow aisle, and then we'll head off
to the bathroom together, leave the occupied sign
unlit, so one by one the passengers
will have to look upon us, unawares,
but be forced to hold their disapproval in abeyance
since we will just be standing in there, clothed
and deciding where we're going to stay
on our honeymoon, joking over how
we forced an entire wedding party
into wearing white, how down the aisle the best man wheeled
your ring to you on a tiny cart (thanks
Tommy), and all the cows sleeping below us
in the pastures as we fly over them, they will lay themselves down
and finally sleep like normal people, without fear
of the rubric of the wolf or the gallows
of their own untenable weight. The earth
is funny that way, not always the receptacle
of monoliths. In the meantime,
though, I'll have a couple of aspirin

and whatever it was that William Blake
was having, and then I'd like to ask the pilot now
if I could be returned to this bit
of airspace again, this one, right there,
it's gone now, so sad: it had that anonymous,
rectangular feeling to it, like a hotel room
or the top of a pool table, and for a just a couple
seconds there — remember? — right before we started dropping
through a bank of clouds topping off Austin
like a barrister's wig, we were happy in it.

Alamo Theory II

Night falling once like a bride
through a roof. Corpse candle
flicking down the marsh-path
and Page God wired into the verity.
Page God considering your mouth
to be American soil, so no matter
the country your mouth arrives in,
Page God shoving all the refugees
inside it. Alamo. Hetero. Halo,
won't we get lonely here
with nothing left but the orgy
alive outside the mouthful? Apologies
to the inhabitants of the condo
next to my condo, for the falling
bride, for scheming on the same
gold as you, for all this terror, for
the imagination like a dentist's
waiting area, and such pliable
teeth you once had, sighing like
anemone, Page God bleaching
his/her pubic hair, so that no one
better even recognize. Him or her:
it is not polite to query: it is going
to set me up in the tallest example
of the watchtowers. No one loves
a lone outpost like I can. No one

wants to see the horde, like I
want to see it, as it comes there
funneling through the valley, cross-
dressed in the hollowed-out
bodies of my fallen comrades. Am
I feeling righteous yet? Daylight,
lying on my back, with ratted-out
entrail, and how come the clouds,
and why feathered back across the sun
like the bangs of mythic swimsuit
models? Chaos theory, how we
loved you, your days of connection
visible, days that followed days,
and the rumor of Page God, like
a parasite glowing in the eye of
the snail, plus there even seemed
a consequence. Go ahead, overrun me,
all you cohesive beings. Gums,
cheek, tongue: there's too much flesh
in the human mouth already.

Here Are Some Problems I Have with Your Wife

I

She's a successful deep-sea mining
operation. A traffic record so clean
you could wash a human heart with it.
When I read your wife's poems, I understand
that it's just the single, immense fish
hiding inside of me, and not millions
of tiny sperm, as biology holds out. Same
thing goes for missiles and economics
in which little ever rhymes. I once met
a girl who, in your wife's company, went
from socialism to only being turned on
by images of Santa Claus. I know
how that goes. Spiny dorsal fin and torched
Xmas stocking. Poetry's not for everyone.

II

I object to the way she has peopled
the earth. When I pull her hair, it spools
hurtless from her scalp, like dental floss.
In the broader world, authorities still try
to outlaw bestiality, and the days all pass,
lit as if adult films, yet with surprisingly
good acting. *If you're what I'm going to have
as my disciple,* your wife once said to me,
then what's my body and my blood

supposed to be? Okay then, but how would
you've replied? When shy in public stalls
and unable to urinate, I breathe deeply,
imagine your wife, singing. This bliss shut
to animals. No codpiece after Labor Day.

III

I imagine, at some point, I read a book
your wife didn't write. Not the Bible, maybe,
but a kind of bible. Or maybe not even
a book, but someone's diary other than
your wife's diary. Have you ever read
your wife's diary? Well I'm not ready
to recommend it. I'm alone, reading in bed,
when your wife's arm bursts through
the grave of my chest, as if buried in me
prematurely, then all of her, shooting
through me, a black firework, into the ceiling.
It's like how it was always rain, but I kept
receiving it as milk, and it's also the way
I wound up written out of everything.

What It's Like Outside

The great detective steps over the corpse and walks across the apartment to the open window, through which the killer's bullets entered the room. Using his pencil as a pointer, he sticks his hand out the window, toward the building across the street, plotting the likely trajectory of the bullets. *There,* he says to the young lieutenant, and *There.* He puts his other hand out the window, just to make sure, and then he pokes his head out, too. Though the forecast said rain, it's a beautiful day, and he stays that way a long time: half in, half out, eyes looking skyward, his pencil upraised like a baton. Soon, on the sidewalk below him, an orchestra begins to form. It seems there will be music after all! The violins appear, carrying folding chairs and music stands, which they arrange according to the great detective's instructions. The cellos shout a greeting to the bassoons, who've just stepped off the downtown bus, and the young lieutenant produces a silver triangle from his pocket. When the lone oboist tests his reed—squink!—one by one the other instruments begin, and this is the great detective's favorite part: the sound of his orchestra warming up, an oblong planet, drifting through space along its weird english. But has anyone seen the first violin? She's never late, she's so talented. Oh there she is! There, crossing the street toward the orchestra, sandals slapping the pavement, her orange rain slicker popping with each step. The great detective smiles as she opens up her battered, black violin case. She's like a daughter to him, and in a moment he'll tap the windowsill with his baton, and finally we in the audience can relax, because we know it's unlikely that anyone was murdered here, what with the first violin accounted for, and it being concert day.

Notes Toward an Imperial Poetry

No more masturbating in the gift shop
No more days dropping like child actors
Days like something Antigone might have buried
Days in which my friend and I hold hands in the street and eat up what the
       palmerworm hath not yet eaten
And watch young people exercise
And remind me what the old evil was, again?
Scrap of flag poking out of the dirt
We must deliver the claw hammer
Annihilator, step into the calendry
Rip off the head and gnaw on the neck peg, as if we are dolls
Where the wages of capitalism are wages
Where puncture to the small beasts who are deserving of it
Snood of the living body with the spirit bursting from its fold as lamprey,
       microscopics from another plane wriggling in its teeth
Where we're bringing King George back
No more darkrooms, no more dressing rooms
Not a doll that pees itself but a doll that pees on other dolls
I did not feel the spirit's anger was anarchic
Your body in the back of every ambulance in New York City
Call of Duty: the Battle of Tel Megiddo
Annihilator, if one wants a mother, one puts a mother
If one wants a father, then one goes ahead and puts one
Third-person-limited omniscient shooter
In the dark of the VIP room Death's going to let us put our little stickies on it
Elegy for it (how you tried to fit it: how you couldn't keep it fit)

And of the even smaller beasts who are deserving of it

And was it Monday's child who was full of hair?

Is lubricant the only apology we'll ever need?

No sundress, for any sex or species, in or around the Annihilator

Antigone's holding hands with her friends in the street and she's sending out the Polaroids

Summer's still the heavy favorite

Parts of the day left scattered behind in motel refrigerators all across the Northeast

Gnostic reviser, time clicking in the horse, voice the departure point of spirit from the flesh,
       and God's assent as my thumb slips to its fit in the jugular notch

Antigone keeping lookout in the whale watch

And all these seaside cottages with photographs of seaside cottages on their bedroom walls

Annihilator, your voice is holy and it goes wherever you go

Do not take it with you into the gift shop

Do not hand its body to the adult acoustics

Death's going to let us put our little stickies on it, one last time

Elegy for it (and how I put it out of my misery: lit it: how it won't stay lit)

One Shies at the Prospect of Raising Yet
Another Defense of Cannibalism

"You can't kiss a movie," Jean-Luc Godard said, and this is mostly true, in that you cannot initiate the kiss. The Movie could initiate the kiss if The Movie wanted, as it is so much taller, leaning in, no way to demur, you would be too polite anyway, and, as the Roman poets have stressed, there is always something porous in the decorous. So there can be kissing between you and The Movie, and it would be amazing, better the more incoherent The Movie is and the more you had to pay to see it, though in the movies it is said that prostitutes don't like to kiss as kissing is too personal, though I disagree, as sometimes the human will make a show of locating you with a kiss, almost to prove to you that you are a real person with a face and that, absolutely, they know where the face is and the face isn't, and this is how you know, for sure, that both of you have been paid. But I don't want to make you feel bad here, and I apologize, for you are entirely kissable, as I have watched you through windows and keyholes even though, up to this point, you do not appear in movies. Often you appear holding a book in your hand and with God knows what playing in your head—I imagine you repeating to yourself, over and again, "the horse knows the way, the horse knows the way"—and remember: even someone as learned in film as Jean-Luc Godard got it a little wrong. You *can* kiss The Movie, if The Movie wants to kiss you. It's just that The Movie, finally, isn't all that interested in your mouth.

One Day, Alone on the Houseboat, Vince Neil Changes
the Name of Everyone He Has Known, Knows, or Is
Like to Know — Male and Female — to James

I, Vince Neil, still white and thus far
unraped, my ancestry so busy
sucking on me that they're
unable to pay attention
to the ritual, am not really worried
about what Giotto
could or would have done
with the color of this particular sky,
nor the too-early moon
clipped to it, crescent and sterilized
like a belly-button ring. As of this minute
I am done being asked
to tell one person from
the next, to qualify near sunset, or to attempt the differentiation
of fish, of shrub, although looking up
the word *lambent*
each time I come upon it
isn't such a bad thing. A word like that,
when it crawls inside you,
seems to have more claws
than demanded by the logic
of evolution, seems like
it should never leave the body
unless pronged out, yet each time I meet it

I am looking at a stranger. I think it's also clear
that I am never speaking
of my own genitalia. You have a lot of claws too,
James, and you are like
America, winner of the Best
Dead Body of the Year Award
for the second year running, arms and heads
at legion, a few of you dressed up
as nurses, no news, as of yet,
whether you are a fool, or to be murdered. A word on nurses: sometimes
they are men, but all of them
were James. A word on James: sometimes
they are ladies, James, trust me, it's hard
to be certain: declination, conjugation, 1989
was the blurred tail of a lion
cutting through the sawgrass
of an unhospitalized landscape,
wan orgasm, the Bambi reaction, fresh
minnows, harpies seen flying over
my dinner table. When I say *we*
I try to use it in the prison sense. Do we
have to imagine that the Sirens
actually sat down and wrote the songs
they were famous for singing? And even with only two
bodies in the bed, still it was difficult
to keep track of all assembled
pieces, doing the human math
over and again, and once in a while,
in my live addition, somehow coming up

with an improbable and third set
of teeth. Courtney Love,
you're the only one I can talk to
about this. I mention distress
to garner effect, but I grew
to like the superfluation, only sensing vaguely sometimes
that the extra set of teeth,
and the rogue face enhousing it, could belong
to a participant ghost,
only sensing vaguely sometimes that the ghosts
could have worrisomely been
long-dead relatives of mine, dressed in their armor
or hats, coming back
and starved for contact, herein
you have already heard me say
strange things about the habits
of my ancestry. Like many of you,
we were a line of decent
sleepers, our pity went out
to abused machines, we tended toward houses
with useless half baths, and if no one should
invade us, then expect egregious behavior
in the international theater. Which
reminds me: if I have to bathe
this body one more time, this my own
right foot for example, one of my hostages
is going to die. A woman, a child, do you call it *foot*
where you come from? Do you dare to call it *kiss*
and do you cry? Geography

concerns me, though I am able to pretend
that I do not know what city's port
I am currently at harbor in, might be interested
in a form of faith where a ghost
could be believed in, but without
the certainty of the afterlife
that the ghost-body, like a road sign, promises. The murder mysteries
keep getting better. Also would like to call you over,
James, with your many pocketknives
inside your many handbags, your line of disagreeing shoes
leading from my bedroom door
to Mars and halfway back. We can hold hands
on a bed bestrewn with all the coupons
you've cut out this week, just like
your mother taught you. Your mother's name is James
and she will eat from anyone's
proffered hand. It was a penis, furthermore,
that could have had a gravel road
leading up to it. And in the cellblock
of this logic, I eventually will have to try
a few things, as poltergeist,
on my own distant progeny, my sad
relatives, not too soon after my death
shall I do so, as that would be
so awful for all of us, but once a few
hundred years have passed,
and my future grandchildren
are living in their hovering tents,
I will attack them in their sleeping bags

with the silt of Mars making
its red tears in my eyes. My living self, though, I don't
need much: an answer to duration, or maybe line up
all of your pretty heads, James,
and speak a chorus while I
am urinating overdecks, make sure to hide
the philosophy book you're reading, later help me
rewrite my personal statement
down at the sperm bank. Boundaries
are necessary. Your aunt, for example, the cyclops
with the denotative worm
in her gut. It's just that sometimes
I get the feeling that, biologically speaking, I am filled
with girls. The gametes
in my possession feel to me
this way, that they are each to build
the distinction of a girl-child, millions of girl-children,
I can see them now, post-
domesticated and lean of mind, so few
of them tattooed
and this giving the totality of their bodies
a baleful silence in the can-light,
call them in free from hide-and-seek
and watch as not one of them
appears, all learning quickly to speak
only when they are killing something,
an army much unlike their father, who was never
very organized, never one soldier
at any one time. Apotheosis is the moment—

and you will all experience it, James —
when you turn into a god
against your will. But if this
is going to be about daughters, I hear
you asking me, then what is it going
to be about? Sometimes, I worry
that the philosophical impulse in me
is a very fine and weapons-grade
nostalgia, that maybe the belief
in a lost system of the past
is the marketplace, one digital telephone
firing on the next, but my sense of time
is mostly emotional, plus don't engage
with fashion anymore, not drinking these days
so I don't have the patience, a necktie,
anyway, is for a hopeful fellow who believes
the villagers will not use it
to strangle him. I do not pity such a man,
though, strangled by brethren,
for he died with love whispering inside of him
like more than one witch. It's a sad thing to think about, James,
but someday Josh, too, will have
to become James. Time? My girls
don't require it, they draw
their stick figures first, and then they get busy
without permission, for all I know
you could be one of them, though I don't think my daughters
would ever be caught
reading this. Once, before

I was famous, I drove from Malibu to Oklahoma
with a woman in possession of a triple row of eyelashes,
stepping forward in each eye, like a rotor
of shark's teeth. They fell out of her head
and marked a black dotted line, down the highway,
so much easier for the killers
and the handshake artists
to follow us, the cacti and landmarks,
as we passed them slowly by, reminding me
of the pictures of food
on laminated menus, so orderly and shining,
but, at last, so disappointing
once we got out of the car
and put our mouths on them. I mention her now
because so far she hasn't yet fit
into any other poem and she
is probably a mother now. That which
does not kill you makes you stronger,
it is said, such as flip-flops
and condoms. If it's done right,
eschatology is the supply-side
in perfect harmony with
demand. So from this point forward
in my rhetorical, all variety of bird to be referred to
as *chicken,* the endless taxonomy of trees
boiled down to *oak,* will try to stop appending trust
to the immanence of the *of,* though very rarely
does a person take the time to handwrite

a personal letter anymore, and clearly this
is the best news we've had
since the rise of alphabets. Happy Mother's Day,
you group of otherwise disparate
individuals. There were wires and insects
in the penmanship, abattoir
through obligation, they would rack up
some spelling for you, and when you sent
your own letter back, it had better be signed
and this was a way for the ones who love you
to better learn to forge your signature,
tyranny of the addressee. Just like the Sirens,
I plan to memorize
the entirety of the Koran. Just like the Sirens, I don't want a lot
of written testament around, and though
it was nice for a while, I also won't be needing
the internet any longer. Stomp
your feet, James. Wave your hands in the air
forever, report your debits
and your wee genetic messagery
into the All. Now, the blank night-chicken
is going to sing its sleep-time song
for us, three repeating notes that I
am not interested in
identifying. As for my dowry, I offer you
only the body surrounding me, gift-wrapped
junction of bone, within which that thing
that you and Nietzsche have taken

to calling a heart, stranger
to industry, medium
percussion, talking bullshit to the future
and with its pants off in the rain.

Yep, I Said *Camel*

In the wanted poster, the famous sunflower rises,
from her cowboy hat, like a periscope. By then,
its roots had tapped into her frontal lobe, drew
her thoughts as nutrients and paid her back
with visions. Through this sunflower eye
she dreamed the endless, lurid H of train tracks,
foretold a scumbag frequency of sheep. And to
my shame, she eavesdropped while the Indians
searched my saddlebags and found the dress
I took from her. Boys, I wore it only once, tucked
the gingham into my gun belt, rode that fucking
camel back to Taos. Whatever I said there, I said
to her, as her. If you like my dress, then keep
your bullets. Keep your bullets. They're no good here.

The Record

Prosecution's objection sustained on grounds of high birth weight, inconvenient understudy, hidden bathroom; courtroom asked to close eyes and imagine the robot love object, misfiring below Accused in autumn leaves, etc.; Judge states that homosociality is *still* the primary evil; final witness for Prosecution now suggesting Accused was critical of finger paintings; Defense speaks for long time — like history class in Egypt — of scatter wire, digitalis, some rumbling that the lending of books is a sexual act; yours truly, court stenographer, remains confused by the intentions of juror number two; calamine and sweat-sock; witness for Defense states Accused's testimony must be laid down early in day before Accused can become patriotic; *if there were fewer of us* opines Accused *we wouldn't die as regularly,* and yours truly asked to read that wisdom back to Court; Accused's statement read back instead as quote *I will run for president on the platform of your bodies;* yours truly now integral part of Justice, considers calling parents; Judge says *if you can get a woman to move from one room to another, it is a victory;* must remember to ask Judge if she is a he or a she, and if a she or a he would he or she let yours truly wear her or his robe sometime: his or her notebook, look you, has a little garter strap on it; some of this had better be political; clock on the wall, sexy like a porthole; Defense says *Your Honor, I can't be bothered, dash of clemency, incipience of clauses;* audience agrees that the keeping of bees is not a sexual act but an act of aggression, casus belli; harpoon and foxtail; Judge known to have spent her or his youth teasing the War-Bird, Jehovah; yours truly asked to read entire record back to Court for no reason than Defense likes my reading voice; *it sounds* quote *like a child's plastic shovel, digging a little grave;* by this time Judge and the Accused k-i-s-s-i-n-g, conflict of haircuts, hysteresis court-wide, *we are not more beautiful than TIME* shouts bailiff, subsequently dismissed; turns out juror number two has a piece of paper stating yours truly is her actual property; *and* is sexy, like a porthole; eventually decided it would be a good idea, for future trials, to have a nurse on hand; last words of the Accused read into record: *in case of Rapture, do not resurrect; forward all DNA to the widows of Arcady.*

Please speak to me
    or if you must
bring up only that
    don't share. I know
thing to ask. Yes, as I
    remarked, shore lunch
was lovely. Your
    stayed put. Later on
do now, pull it from
    as if for final proof
sleeping with
    picnics of the past
such things. The rock,
    we sat, ran beneath
the same rock we
    over to the other
felt, believe me,
    two people. *Person,*
have said, *hold on.*
    the name we had
your fault. A name
    with the blankness
feeling in regard
    for saying this

only of the present
    bring up the past
which you and I
    this is a selfish
have often
    at hanging rock
hair and mine
    we didn't, as we
each other's clothes
    that we've been
each other. In the glorious
    we simply knew
upon which
    the lake, and was
were both looking
    side at. I almost
as if we were
    I nearly could
Instead, I used
    agreed upon. Not
is useful, it helps
    I am sometimes
to you. I apologize
    out loud. You are not

What do you think?

BOOK TITLE: _____

COMMENTS: _____

_____

_____

_____

_____

OUR MISSION:

Poetry is vital to language and living. Copper Canyon Press publishes extraordinary poetry from around the world to engage the imaginations and intellects of readers.

Thank you for your thoughts!

Can we quote you? ☐ yes ☐ no

☐ Please send me a catalog full of poems and email news on forthcoming titles, readings, and poetry events.

☐ Please send me information on becoming a patron of Copper Canyon Press.

NAME: _____

ADDRESS: _____

CITY: _____ STATE: _____ ZIP: _____

EMAIL: _____

MAIL THIS CARD, SHARE YOUR COMMENTS ON FACEBOOK OR TWITTER,
OR EMAIL POETRY@COPPERCANYONPRESS.ORG

Copper Canyon Press
A nonprofit publisher dedicated to poetry

 CopperCanyonPress.org

BUSINESS REPLY MAIL
FIRST-CLASS MAIL   PERMIT NO. 43   PORT TOWNSEND WA

POSTAGE WILL BE PAID BY ADDRESSEE

Copper Canyon Press
PO Box 271
Port Townsend, WA 98368-9931

NO POSTAGE
NECESSARY
IF MAILED
IN THE
UNITED STATES

the blankness
      of. Plug your thought
into me, and it
      fail to light. You are
what I mean about
      despite my facility
for detail, may not
      your name? I am
will run us through
      pull our way
if only to see, at last,
      of the spear-grip.
as a topic, is sadly
      cast the deep side
together. The lake
      we scrape across
the weed tops,
      flags, above
settlements, the castle
      your hooks
how destructive
      so go ahead
against them,
      against time,
that swim. Our fiber-
      burnt orange;
of shining gold;
      somewhere in the lake

I am speaking
      or daydream
or I will often
      beginning to see
the past, how I,
      with pliers, and eye
be suitable. What was
      not kidding. What comes
from the front, we
      down its length
what has ahold
      Therefore, the future,
also out. Instead, let's
      of the weed bed
is black, like slate
      with paddles toward
sticking up, like alien
      the invisible
you've dropped
      inside of. I love
you are with the fishes,
      and bring your war
against the duck,
      against all things
glass canoe is of
      our shapely hooks
our giant rock, also
      beneath us, is

the bottom, toward
    lip-hooked, dives
its weight a thing
    to follow, as if
both for what we had
    we didn't want

which the minnow,
    after the lead,
the minnow seems
    we sent it dropping
to give away and still
    the lake to have.

The Creature

Like many humans, I enjoy lifting small, living things. Your wife qualifies, but doesn't like to be lifted. I guess it's probably because, as is true with many humans, your wife doesn't want to be eaten, and often we are lifted, by the bigger thing, right before it drops us on a rock and eats us. *I understand,* I say to your wife, lowering her body to the kitchen floor, her legs bending slowly as she takes back the weight I've returned to her, like an astronaut moving back into the gravity of the capsule. *The captain,* I say, *should go down with her ship. But Janine and Kim,* your wife says, *must go down on each other.* And who are Janine and Kim? And how many times over, as if I were a country of phone-sex operators, should I be asked to lose my innocence, Taurus ensorcelled by the crab, birthstone Gomorrah? Now your wife takes my hand, as if she's overheard this thought, and we turn to look out the window at the city, length after length of sheer brown light, like panty hose, slipping over the faces of the buildings below, plus the single, just visible bolt-end of the moon. If somewhere, down there, on this new planet, with its lone moon and sun, there were a human big enough to lift me, like I was the child it had searched for and found, I know how afraid I would have to be, looking up into that face. I think your wife much less afraid than that when she is lifted, and this makes me want to pick her up again, shake her body until I disconnect the arms from the body, as then she could no longer lift me with them if someday she grew tall enough to lift me, but I do not. It seems as if Janine and Kim are starting to like this moon a little better: no sister or brother, no caretaker, it has a certain dignity, looked at like an actress and comfortably dead. Like many of you humans,

I enjoy lifting small, living things, because sometimes they fear me, because I could save them if I needed to, and this is a powerful feeling if you haven't known it, and also what the creature will accept as love.

Vince Neil's Report to the Malibu City Chamber of Commerce,
in Which He Refuses, and Finally Agrees, to Make a Journey to
the Underworld to Visit with the Known and Unknown Dead

1

Baby. Adult. But where's the next
round of teeth, for the meat
that lies ahead? The pharmacology
to get us through
the last aubade? The keeper
of the epic checklist
writ in red? You hope
that watching my arc
is going to sync you
tight to Time
and all its webbing? And who are you
out there saying

2

that the language
is still your friend? Have you not felt it
turning between your knees? Yet it is not
a horse. Have you not felt it
roiling in the deeps
or heard it charging
for you through the reeds? Yet it is not
Leviathan, as first we suspected, the thing

3

where only God
could make it sing, could hook it
through the nose and make it sing. Stay
undoable, Malibu, your hunger
turning into sleep. If ever they say to you
that the song they're going to sing
will save you,
it only means that they're about
to be irrelevant. Put, instead,
your faith in me, irrelevant
upon arrival, oh be fruitful
but do not multiply. From left to right,
even as it's moving now,
even as it is appearing in a book,
this was all written on a rock
for you, by you, and it's just my hand
got stuck here in the middle
of it somehow. Eating the cow
teaches you that you are not the cow, but when you eat the human being
you learn nothing.
Come with me
and learn nothing. No systemic
for Malibu. Just the singular, pure thought
like a lone guard shack on a border
and all the cars and trucks
come pulling up to it
barely having to prove the existence

of the faces, riding there inside, a little like
but most unlike
the sempiternal minute
that I am wearing out
even as I speak to you: thirty seconds
into the future
and still I can see you,
still watch the car-wreck
and the forehead kisses
coming on, me hunching forward
in the bubble, periscope high in the meridian
of the minute, so
I'm going to lose you
once you've drifted thirty seconds
into the back stream, victim
of jurisdiction, will try to float back to you
a valentine from time
to time, addressed my dear
anonymous. My dear
anonymous, like the shepherds, will you not
put an engine in me? Anonymous,
the dead might talk about you
on their blogs, but they're talking about me
in their sleep. Anonymous,
either come back to me carrying
this shield, or come back to me
with your dead body being carried
upon this shield, but either way,
you know I'm going to want

my motherfucking shield back. In China
they built entire cities in which millions of people
could live, and they are now
and have always been
standing empty, train lines running out
through mica flats
to nobody, not ghost towns
because no one has ever lived there
or died as the symptom
of a personal betrayal, which is exactly how
I founded Malibu
when I founded it. The objection
to the underworld
is also crowds. Same with heaven,
where the angels are lovely,
but when we see one
at the airport in Cleveland
lying belly-down at the end of the escalator,
with its mouth gaping open,
we are sore afraid
and know very well that minute-present
is our only module
of time: you can feel that minute, elongating
and used, overtouched, seen from every
inhospitable angle, packed
from both ends
by limitless
emptiness, just like you
who do not pilot it, packed

from both ends,
and seen from every angle, the human figure
with a mirror for skin, and there will never be
the change
promised coming, your toes pointing
with their magnetism
in the direction
of the nearest clock. Angel wings
owe too much to the bat-skin
anyway. It's that
feeling you get in the movie theater
when a character on-screen
is named the name
that is your name. They're calling for you
but it's not yours to answer. For a while
that name was real
but then it got
kept real. Did you see the ghosts
in your childhood home? At first
I wasn't scared, thought it a privilege
to grow up
in the middle of someone's
desperate afterlife
acted out in playroom
and a kitchen
no longer
belonged to. And did you see the bombs?
When they fell on me
they fell on nothing. Malibu, it was you

I saw there, taking your belt off,
too slowly, for airport security, just this side
of the demonstrative, watched you shuffle
through the gates
as the uniformed stranger, in another room
invisible to you,
went sorting through
your clothing
and your gifts. Whatever you had
in there, considered dangerous,
liquid with sunlight, it already
expired, or it blew up
years ago. What time is it, now?
the Sirens ask you. The Sirens,
which I mentioned
in another poem
that Josh cut from this book,
are my true daughters, and every time my daughters sing to me
the seductive songs that tear
the heart away from the aerie of the mind
it gets a little awkward
for everyone
involved. Incest, please
reject me. What time is it, now?
again the Sirens ask, and you'll want to say
it's four in the morning, reader, because
it feels like four in the morning, but it's not four
in the morning yet, time still

4

working on its game. You know very well
it's still the same time
it was when we started
all of this, baby, adult, spring being
the last cyclical thing
we didn't know to laugh at, the American season
of tall birds and first aid, thunder
or an air conditioner kicking on
somewhere in the un-
motorcycled dawn, down
a season, season
down, Malibu
down, Leviathan
down, the pilgrim's
incandescent member
passing like a smokestack
across the banquet table,
as if in blessing, and lastly,
the clouds of the Pacific sky
creeping into our lungs again,
where they take the shape
of sad animals
bent on revenge. Leviathan, here
are the warlikes and the ladylikes.
Leviathan, what's my sea level now?
I really never minded
engulfment as a death, total

rearrangement, redistribution. It is shameful to leave the evidence
that you operated, once, a shape,
to leave the shape looking so much like you
that others could point to a photo of you
and say it was you
indeed who lived. The family, however,
does not agree. In addition
to the photos, they will demand
as their right
the trophy of the body, to put a stone upon
or wrap in string, to point at it
with love, and when the body
is missing, the family goes
on television,
where it is pictured
as it does not rest. But my love for you

5

is stronger than that, Malibu. The word *ineffable*
means that no one will sleep with you
and that you also can't
be worded in, at which point death
is only the ending
of the few feelings
we were not embarrassed enough
to have. The Sirens, who are my daughters
and who sing to me
in a way that makes me uncomfortable,
aren't hoping to see anything

when they stand there, looking out
across the sea. My love for you
is as strong as that. It will turn its back
politely, but not coldly,
when it's time for you to take your place
in the audience of the dead. Like a French
screen actress. Like a filthy
love between old soldiers. Like
a handclap, rising up
suddenly out of the second verse
in a joyful manner, which suggests
a way to reorganize your life. Who doesn't want to cross over
and then cross back, to hold
your biographer's heart
smoking in your hands? Incest,
I am beginning to see
things differently. We broke
so many covenants together, unruly

6

in the thatch of Genesis, that maybe we
were the Leviathan
God kept speaking of, just
in code, like as in
the metaphor, never content
with simple warmth, hammering
into the glass with our hardship
of a brain, worn cornerless

and focused like a meteor. But enough
with the song, and enough
with the trophy. I would have rather been a vampire
who never learned
to read, or some other
illiterate bird
not known for its voice, hummingbird
but immortal, uninventable,
and filling up
with human blood. I don't want to look
at any photographs, but if I have to, I will only look at photographs
of those people who are currently
alive. Furthermore, I will only look at photographs
of those people who are currently alive
and also sitting in this room with me.
If you are not sitting in this room with me
it is possible you are dead.
If you are dead, don't send me your photographs,
as they will be deleted. This decree
solves all our problems
except the problem of the present, the place
where the engineers have caused for us
sense-past and sense-future,
which are the other problems
that we've just now solved,
but keep popping up like Victorian ghosts
and are essentially lies to get you

out-of-doors, the present clearly
the blossom point

8

of the serial ill. Have you attended a picnic
that didn't end in tears? And do
you want your shield back, now? No, I don't
want my shield back. I never liked trying to fall
asleep each night, and I voted
every day. You can keep
the moon too, which no one else
would think of farming, not in this semi-
urban setting, one flattened
chorus frog on the sidewalk, the Circle K following me
from city to city. I never
really owned these trees, either,
but still I could try
to pass them on to you, along with the mail
of the mailbox,
plus the stars stalling out,
and all the young parents
lost in the Cineplex. And in order
to further do away
with the present, likewise none
who are living
may approach me in my offices

without a photograph of their face
taped over their face, and I
will also tape a photograph of my face
over my real face, predicate imprint

inadmissible. Photoface, please won't you sit next to me
here in my offices? Photoface, of course
I will sit here next to you. Photoface, thank you
for bringing back my shield. Photoface, I really think
you're going to need
your shield, can already hear
the audience of the dead
rustling like a great, canvas fish
on the deck, audience of the dead
like a ring of gray pollen
chanting *body, body, body,*
you know
they'd all be chanting *body,* foreworld
and afterworld
hardly a given, and tied
to the centerworld,
which is the feeder graft
for the wing-skin
of the invisible. Wow, you're really

11

speaking my language, Photoface. Often,
and in a manner
that suggests it's a compliment, the lover will tell you
how they're going to make you feel
like you're the only human being
on Earth. No mother, no father, no friends. And sometimes
you will be asked to sit down
to eat of a food
that comes in a container
likewise made of food. Surprise. It was you
who were the object
all this time, and this makes of you
a kind of god. Happy birthday

12

Photoface. Since I can't tell for sure
whether or not
the photograph
that you've taped over your face
actually matches your face
there below it, it worries me
that you might be the kind of person
who would trick me
into looking at the photograph
of someone's face
who is no longer living. Would you trick me
with the trick

of the photograph
of a dead face
taped over the living face? Or conversely
would you tape the photograph
of a living face
over your dead face
if your face were dead
and you dared to bring it with you

13

into my offices? Would you choose this way
of all the available ways
to lie? These are the kinds of questions
I don't want answered. Stones
of the coast, unmind me. Condor,
float your shadow like a submarine
across our bellies, and if I've forgotten
an addressee or two, just try to hold on
for a short while longer. It was complex
when there was light on it, but the thing you are the god of
is mostly over now.

Complaint

The best fever had a brick for genitals
and it was an effective fever. We
don't want to seem ungrateful for the
having had of such a fever. Likewise
the heart in the kitchen of its chest. And
from time to time, a person walked up
and asked us if we knew directions either
to the cinema or bed. Usually
we did. We were not a lowly bug or even
something simple to be fooled at. The earth
was known as round by us. We had a share
of sex in the movie theater with that
one lost person, whether him or her is not
on the list of our present complaint. A person
it was, in need of directions, which we
often knew of, a person with the fever
that had the faces on it, and this was enough
for happiness. It's just, and we hate
to mention it, but there was the problem
of our heads not growing back
after we had cut them off of each other
or ourselves, tenderly, in the bedroom
with our lost person, turning to each other
after a long day, helping to cut off
each other's head in the accustomed
manner, and fully believing we would

see each other again, but of course we learned
too late that there would only be
the cutting off of heads that once.
Why did you fix it with the single
decapitation? I know what you're thinking
but this is not a bid for immortality.
We don't want to live forever, like bugs
or something simple to be fooled at. The coming
fever, the one just ahead with a number
for genitals, is far too beautiful. We don't
want to live forever. It's only
that we'd like to die more often.

Alamo Theory III

Night falling once like a brick
through a hearse. Page God
making cagey moves toward unilateral
asphyxiation. Page God not
the only one thinking my banality
is hot. Loved one so small can slip
both hands into the mouth, tie
a leash around the uvula, walk
you down to the marketplace,
where you may purchase one
last human slave. Commerce
soon to be suspended. Grief
is the sex halo, but sadly, only those
playing at the highest of levels
will know to undress you
when you're weeping. What could
it be said to mean, when my human
slaves rebel, when my ejaculate
keeps becoming a flock of actual
sparrows? Silly other, retroactive
continuity bolts you to the frame, flesh
without thought, screwing the sternum
down to the spine, until it's easier
not to breathe, or better not to look,
not with your eye into my eye.
For whom are we to be drilling?

And if you're such a good person,
then what were so many sparrows
doing in your basement? If the will
is still what I think it is, then every
decision is an abduction, and the voice
I'm always hearing in the wilderness
is anatomically correct. Page God,
the blood battery. Page God, who never
learns, one thing falling through
one thing. But it's not all downside,
ladies and gentlemen. There are trees,
that rainbow is nothing to be afraid of,
and when I torture you, at least
you won't be thinking about money.

Hidden Lake

The Killer killed the last three girlfriends I brought to sleepaway camp, so it is with a level of sadness, in your parents' kitchen, that I watch you roll up your purple sleeping bag and fill your tin canteen. Why did you have to wear the secondhand safari shorts, today of all days? Why did you make such a big deal of entrusting me with the silver compass your father gave you so you won't get lost in the woods? On the street out-side, I can hear the bus, waiting to take us away. I want to say that you are my favorite so far, so confident, sometimes with the tube-sox, and when you were young, your invisible friend was a girl who looked like you, who shared your first and last names, but never said the word *yes*. I'm going to miss both of you. I don't know why I keep going back to that place by the lake where so many people I love have died. I don't know why I don't open my mouth, right now, to warn you to keep your eyes open around the boathouse, or tell you of the trail through the pine woods that leads to the safety of the highway and that only I know. Yes, you'll want to bring a swimsuit, but I'm sure flashlights will be pro-vided. So many summers I've paused alone, breathless on that path, with the Killer and the screams of the campfire behind me, distraught then, as ever, by how often I've arranged to be alive.

Superwhite

First, there was a fish. And then
there was the consciousness of robots.
What came between
seemed durable enough: history
with no shadow in its mouth, the trees
a medium gorgeous,
and the bodies of shepherd friends
spaced out like picnics
beneath the adage of the sun.
Lord, did I weary of sexing them?
Lord, how I wearied of sexing them,
and of chasing their pronoun
into, and out of, the woods. One day soon
our new robot masters
will all commit suicide. I heard them whispering
their sad plan in the alley. Sorry, playgirl.
You too, playboy. No one's going to take
this time off our hands, after all.

Vince Neil's *Apologia Pro Vita Sua,* as Transcribed by Josh,
in a Crowded Hotel Bar One Afternoon, Being a Poem Spoken
in the Future, During the Upcoming AWP Conference of 2018, in
Tampa, Florida

1

Of the latter heroes I was most
supine, handed out
warnings to women who were pregnant
or were likely to become pregnant,
hope tucked bloodless
into saddlebag, neither hunter
nor borrower, sometimes
referred to myself as *it*—
as in *charity is*
its bird machine—a strap-on fashioned
out of bits of the foregone cross
coming at me from the future
in the tiniest and the most
lineal of dreams, my preferred
haruspex pondering
her retirement and my new
address as quickly
dirty as the last, in times of war
immune to alarum,
at least fifteen minutes away
from sword and armor, the valves of my heart
opening and closing slowly

like the wings of a new butterfly
at rest upon the battlements
of overweening Troy, and all
the maidens and immortals

2

and the handful of princes who,
in those days, took time away
from their own troubled narratives
to stop and save me from myself or from
the ancient Boy Scout Death
are now themselves long dead
by natural and/or
mythological causes. *Don't mention it*
they seemed to say with their great
careful bodies
as they turned them from me in departure.
Don't mention it and drifted leonine
and smooth toward the assault
on their promised
constellations and perhaps
the foreign-funded rebellions
of their homicidal children,
got upon or beneath majestic animals
and graduate students, ears crisp
but not always white
as snow. And where was I — year
of the jellyfish, Cossacked,

bowing feastless
before capital — when they
in their turn required me

3

and I heard them cry out for me
from the dust that their fallen bodies made
in the dust, even better
and taller destroyers looking down
upon them, their lives an endnote
of snuffed-out goat bone, free-range
angels slumped out
on conveyor belts, felled
by slotting bolt in a rusty hank
of factory-light, and by the transitive property
and a million miles away
a flower of blood popping
from the dashboard
of my Camaro? No you haven't

4

heard all this before,
dirtlings. Moreover
there's something not quite real
about sex dolls. They can't
be strangled to death

5

and the conditions for such
an act, the aura of its chance, like
gravity, makes the minimalism
of the vestibule
a possibility. If you don't like
the vestibule, then what about
the service elevator, where tonight we'll strangle
down so easily? Also, the zombie prostitutes
and hustlers, who have lain up
like sandwiches
for hours beneath heat lamps
in order to trick me, with their customized
temperature, that they are living beings to kiss
when they arrive at my hotel door
is one of those bad dreams
spoken of above. In those days
of the dream, and of the various
kingdoms of conscience, I was set on taking
only baths, as in the shower
it was too easy to cry
over the specifications, and kept track
of war and politics
as one does the deeds
of distant cousins. *Who's the blond*
is what I said to myself, then, when I saw
my picture, for the first time
in the record store, wearing my stage clothes
and the wig of Viking witch

6

on the cover of the first album
and winking back up
into my face. It was the me
before, it was the me
pictured, and then it was the me
confused and aching for me
after realizing I was me, that *it*
was me, that charity was
its bird machine, that its soul
had been lifted from out of its body
as if borne up between
the teeth of a giant
black wolf. Like a lot of goddesses
I spent much of my youth
avoiding rape. It wasn't a soul, really,
but how else, like a penitent, to talk
about the way the wolf
was eating it? I don't think it's true
that you owe a debt to those
who've saved your life, that your life is theirs
until the favor is returned. The chance
at favor rarely comes
unless you're in the movie
of favor, and no matter, as once
someone saves you
they can no longer exist
truly for you, you a check
in the win column, it is like they are suddenly

7

a whale now, shooting between
exoplanets, it is like making out
with a galleon, it's a problem to have
a decent conversation or a lunch
with those who have
delivered you. If you're not into
the vestibule, then what do you think
about the Holy Roman Empire? And when
the witch says *be you full of Jove*
then be you full of Jove. Don't make me repeat myself
in front of the poets. Who doesn't like to stay

8

the same size forever
and in successive contexts, so much better
the love object dead
than alive and unable to speak to me normally
in the manner of things
that marry with the other things
and without debit? I can't go on, Josh,
unless I'm told if that bartender
is a woman or what? And this is also why
I will refuse to save the rest of you,
you Richard and you Rachel, notebook
holstered, chipping like you said
at the idiom. But also I would
like to focus on another you, that's right

9

you with the feather in your teeth out there, you
breathing in the dark beyond
the mise-en-page, future you, maybe living
in the lunar colonies, where you weigh
the pros and cons of making war
against the empire
of the planet Earth. You don't
want to pay your taxes either,
and you are fortunate
to be reading this, thumbing it open in front
of your face, holding inside your chest
and hidden far from my eyes
the vulnerable power-core
of your secret wished-fors, time's
quilted darling, why are you so strong
out there at the edge of minutes

10

looking back at me
so dead? You vivid
and gazing out of the bright, blue windows
of Castle Fuck-Me, you considering all of this distraction
as if it is wristwatches
or the faces of the swept-
of-fish-free-seas of your former
home the earth. You are all
that can be thought of, like a wedding reception

after the bride and groom
have retired for the night, so dangerous
and explicit. It's not paranoia. The entire universe
is out to get you pregnant. Ramona, Ramona,

11

why is it me
pretending to be Josh
this time around? Josh, writing up
his inaugural poem. Josh

12

in the kitchen
with usura. I can feel it, the blood he donated
to me, yesterday, in the blood-
mobile, that blood skipping new
like a little colt inside me. Some people believe
that the name we give
to the planet Earth
is too plain, but the plainness of the title
makes the planet easier to miss. Another strategy
is to wear the same clothes, like
a uniform, day after day, so that those days
seem like one day
that will never end. You won't believe it,
but I used to be alive
outside books, in a life that crossed
uncomprehendingly
between two centuries:

in the first century, some things happened
that were too far away
and in the second, some things happened
that were too close. And once in there,
when I was young, more hungry
than patient, I thought I bit into
a carrot stick, but instead
and growling bit into my finger, both predator
and prey. Shame is a big part
of being eaten alive, and because of it
I have been dining at home now
for 1,001 nights, not mature enough,
conceptually, to have
any dealings with the true
human body. Now I think you're getting a better sense
of what my being is. Yes, Officer, I was angry.
All life not within my immediate survey
was a lie. Little horse, little horses,

13

I swear the earth
was still breathing when I left it.

ACKNOWLEDGMENTS

The Awl: "If Not Princess, Then Warden," "The Last Critique," and "Vince Neil (*Apologia Pro Vita Sua*)"

Boston Review: "Complaint"

Columbia: A Journal of Literature and Art: "Alamo Theory," "PSA," and "Your Prime Minister Speaks"

Dossier: "Vince Neil (Open Letter to Malibu)"

Fanzine: "Pensées of the Sucker MC"

The Greensboro Review: "Alamo Theory II"

The Harvard Advocate: "Dollar Dollar Bill"

Harvard Gazette: "Hidden Lake"

Hyperallergic: "Blue Safari"

jubilat: "Here Are Some Problems I Have with Your Wife," "Here Are Some Problems I Have with Your Wife," and "Penultimate Letter to Your Wife"

LIT: "Josh II: *The Return of Josh*" and "Vince Neil (Love Song)"

The Manchester Review: "American History" and "Vince Neil (Cell Phone)"

Narrative: "Alamo Theory III," "Notes Toward an Imperial Poetry," and "Superwhite"

The New Republic: "Where the *I* Comes From"

The New Yorker: "Sci-Fi Violence"

Ninth Letter: "Yep, I Said *Camel*"

Poets.org: "One Shies at the Prospect of Raising Yet Another Defense of Cannibalism" and "*Our Bed Is Also Green*"

A Public Space: "The Creature"

Salt Hill: "The Record"

The Seattle Review: "Vince Neil (Chamber of Commerce)"

Tin House: "Vince Neil (Alone on the Houseboat)"

TriQuarterly: "Vince Neil (Chinese Restaurant)," "We Will Begin by Placing You in This Bag," and "What It's Like Outside"

The Vince Neil poems are dedicated to Matt Guenette, whose idea Vince Neil was in the first place.

Thank you to the faculty and students of Columbia University. Thank you to Lucie Brock-Broido for the example of Lucie Brock-Broido. Thank you to the Sewanee Writers' Conference. Thank you to Don Bogen, Jim Cummins, John Drury, and Michael Griffith at the University of Cincinnati. Thank you Sasha Fletcher and Kate Jenkins for ideas and edits, and to Anton Khodakov for helpful medical terminology. Thank you to Erin Belieu, Mark Bibbins, Jericho Brown, Tim Donnelly, Tim Earley, Kimberly Johnson, and Cate Marvin for their help all along. Thank you to the faculty and students of Harvard University. Thank you to Jorie Graham for the chance. Thank you to Christopher Shipman for keeping my fight record 0-0. Thank you to comrade Dorla McIntosh, always. Thank you to Frank Bell and Susie Sharp for the love and support and the meals. Thank you to Marilyn Bell for the love and support and the meals. Thank you to Doug and Donna Weise for the use of the easy chair in which many of these poems were written. Lastly, thank you to Jillian Weise for the eight million ideas.

ABOUT THE AUTHOR

Josh Bell attended the University of Iowa Writers' Workshop, where he was a Teaching-Writing Fellow and a Paul Engle Postgraduate Fellow. His PhD is from the University of Cincinnati—where he held a Distinguished Graduate fellowship—and he received the Diane Middlebrook fellowship from the University of Wisconsin's Institute for Creative Writing and the Walter E. Dakin fellowship from the Sewanee Writers' Conference. The author of a previous collection of poems, *No Planets Strike,* Bell has been a member of the creative writing faculty at Columbia University and is currently Briggs-Copeland Lecturer, on English, at Harvard University. He has had poems recently published in *The Awl, Boston Review, The New Republic, The New Yorker,* and *Tin House,* as well as in the anthologies *Legitimate Dangers* (Sarabande), *Third Rail: The Poetry of Rock and Roll* (MTV Books), and *Before the Door of God: An Anthology of Devotional Poetry* (Yale). He lives in Cambridge, Massachusetts.

Lannan Literary Selections

For two decades Lannan Foundation has supported the publication and distribution of exceptional literary works. Copper Canyon Press gratefully acknowledges their support.

LANNAN LITERARY SELECTIONS 2016

Josh Bell, *Alamo Theory*

Maurice Manning, *One Man's Darkness*

Paisley Rekdal, *Imaginary Vessels*

Brenda Shaughnessy, *So Much Synth*

Ocean Vuong, *Night Sky with Exit Wounds*

RECENT LANNAN LITERARY SELECTIONS FROM
COPPER CANYON PRESS

James Arthur, *Charms Against Lightning*

Mark Bibbins, *They Don't Kill You Because They're Hungry, They Kill You Because They're Full*

Malachi Black, *Storm Toward Morning*

Marianne Boruch, *Cadaver, Speak*

Jericho Brown, *The New Testament*

Olena Kalytiak Davis, *The Poem She Didn't Write and Other Poems*

Michael Dickman, *Green Migraine*

Kerry James Evans, *Bangalore*

Tung-Hui Hu, *Greenhouses, Lighthouses*

Deborah Landau, *The Uses of the Body*

Sarah Lindsay, *Debt to the Bone-Eating Snotflower*

Lisa Olstein, *Little Stranger*

Camille Rankine, *Incorrect Merciful Impulses*

Roger Reeves, *King Me*

Richard Siken, *War of the Foxes*

Ed Skoog, *Rough Day*

Frank Stanford, *What About This: Collected Poems of Frank Stanford*

For a complete list of Lannan Literary Selections from Copper Canyon Press, please visit Partners on our website:
www.coppercanyonpress.org

Poetry is vital to language and living. Since 1972, Copper Canyon Press has published extraordinary poetry from around the world to engage the imaginations and intellects of readers, writers, booksellers, librarians, teachers, students, and donors.

WE ARE GRATEFUL FOR THE MAJOR SUPPORT PROVIDED BY:

THE PAUL G. ALLEN FAMILY FOUNDATION

Anonymous
Donna and Matt Bellew
John Branch
Diana Broze
Janet and Les Cox
Beroz Ferrell & The Point, LLC
Mimi Gardner Gates
Alan Gartenhaus and Rhoady Lee
Linda Gerrard and Walter Parsons
Gull Industries, Inc.
    on behalf of William and Ruth True
Mark Hamilton and Suzie Rapp
Carolyn and Robert Hedin
Steven Myron Holl
Lakeside Industries, Inc.
    on behalf of Jeanne Marie Lee

Maureen Lee and Mark Busto
Brice Marden
Ellie Mathews and Carl Youngmann as
    The North Press
H. Stewart Parker
Penny and Jerry Peabody
John Phillips and Anne O'Donnell
Joseph C. Roberts
Cynthia Lovelace Sears and
    Frank Buxton
The Seattle Foundation
Kim and Jeff Seely
David and Catherine Eaton Skinner
Dan Waggoner
C.D. Wright and Forrest Gander
Charles and Barbara Wright

The dedicated interns and faithful volunteers of Copper Canyon Press

TO LEARN MORE ABOUT UNDERWRITING COPPER CANYON PRESS TITLES, PLEASE CALL 360-385-4925 EXT. 103

The Chinese character for poetry is
made up of two parts: "word" and
"temple." It also serves as pressmark
for Copper Canyon Press.

The text is set in Baskerville 10,
a digital reworking of the eighteenth-
century type of John Baskerville by
František Štorm. Titles are set in
Berthold Akzidenz Grotesk.
Book design and composition by
VJB/Scribe. Printed on archival-
quality paper.